D1306026

Koala
Commotion

Story by Rebecca Johnson
Photos by Steve Parish

GARETH**STEVENS**
GS
P U B L I S H I N G
A Member of the WRC Media Family of Companies

Please visit our web site at: www.garethstevens.com
For a free color catalog describing Gareth Stevens Publishing's list of high-quality books
and multimedia programs, call 1-800-542-2595 (USA) or 1-800-387-3178 (Canada).
Gareth Stevens Publishing's fax: (414) 332-3567.

Library of Congress Cataloging-in-Publication Data

Johnson, Rebecca, 1966–
    [Koala's big day]
    Koala commotion / story by Rebecca Johnson; photos by Steve Parish. — North American ed.
        p. cm. — (Animal storybooks)
    Summary: When news spreads among the koalas that there will be a special event, a baby koala
convinces his mother that they should attend.
    ISBN 0-8368-5972-3 (lib. bdg.)
    1. Koala—Juvenile fiction. [1. Koala—Fiction.] I. Parish, Steve, ill. II. Title.
    PZ10.3.J683Ko   2005
    [E]—dc22   2005042875

First published as *Koala's Big Day* in 2002 by Steve Parish Publishing Pty Ltd, Australia.
Text copyright © 2002 by Rebecca Johnson. Photos copyright © 2002 by Steve Parish Publishing.
Series concept by Steve Parish Publishing.

This U.S. edition first published in 2006 by
Gareth Stevens Publishing
A Member of the WRC Media Family of Companies
330 West Olive Street, Suite 100
Milwaukee, Wisconsin 53212 USA

This edition copyright © 2006 by Gareth Stevens, Inc.

Gareth Stevens series editor: Dorothy L. Gibbs
Gareth Stevens cover and title page designs: Dave Kowalski

Printed in the United States of America

1 2 3 4 5 6 7 8 9 09 08 07 06 05

When
the koalas
heard the news,
they came
from everywhere!

There were
koalas with coats
of light-colored fur

and koalas with coats
of dark-colored fur.

5

There were
curious
young koalas

and wise
old koalas.

They all stopped to listen
as the news spread
through the bush.

When
baby koala
heard
the news,

he asked
his mother,
"Can we go?"

"It's far away,"
said mother koala.

"You will have
to hang on
very tight."

The excited baby koala climbed aboard his mother's back — and off they went.

On the way,
they met
a lazy old koala,
lounging between
two tree branches.

"Do you want to come with us?"
asked baby koala.

"Not today,"
said the old koala.
"I'm much too tired."

"You go,
then tell me
all about it
when you
get back."

The baby koala
and his mother
moved on
until they reached
an enormous
eucalyptus tree
covered with
fresh, green leaves.

As they
climbed
the tree,
they heard
a shout.

"Hello, there! Come and join the fun."

In the trees around them,
there were koalas everywhere.
It was a koala party!

And there were plenty of tasty leaves
for everyone. Baby koala even picked
some leaves to take home
to the old koala.

It had been a very exciting day.